STRANGE BUT TRUE STORIES

BOOK 3

Phantom Ships

The Jersey Devil

Living Dinosaurs?

...and More!

Janet Lorimer

SADDLEBACK
EDUCATIONAL PUBLISHING

STRANGE BUT TRUE STORIES

Property Of
Wisconsin School for the Deaf

32000123708788

SADDLEBACK
EDUCATIONAL PUBLISHING
www.sdlback.com

ISBN-13: 978-1-61651-767-0
ISBN-10: 1-61651-767-0
eBook: 978-1-61247-298-0

Printed in Malaysia

20 19 18 17 16   7 8 9 10 11

CONTENTS

STRANGE BUT TRUE STORIES

THE JERSEY DEVIL

"Oh, no, a flat tire!" the taxicab driver groaned. He steered his cab to the side of the road and looked around. He shivered slightly in the silence. There wasn't another house for miles in this lonely part of the New Jersey countryside. And there were no other cars on the road. The scary creature everyone was calling the Jersey Devil flashed into his mind.

"Stop that nonsense!" he told himself crossly. "The sooner you get the tire changed, the sooner you'll get out of here." He quickly went to work.

He was about to put the jack back in the trunk when he heard a shrill scream! Looking up, he gasped in horror. A hideous creature was flying toward him! He left the jack and the tire behind as he dove into the back seat.

Then the monster landed on the roof

and the car rocked violently. Letting out another piercing scream, the creature rocked the cab back and forth. Was it trying to rip off the roof?

The cab driver decided to start the car. But he was shaking so badly, he was afraid he'd flood the engine. "Oh, please," he begged silently, "please start."

Suddenly, the engine roared to life, and the creature let go. As it rose into the sky, the driver cringed as he heard a final angry scream.

The jack and the damaged tire were left behind as the driver sped away.

* * *

That cab driver encountered the Jersey Devil back in 1929. And that was just one of many documented sightings. All across the state people were asking the same question: Is the Jersey Devil a hallucination, a mythical creature . . . or is it some kind of biological freak? Written records say it's been around for more than 200 years. And the creature's been seen by more than 2,000 people.

The Jersey Devil was first spotted in 1735. At that time, some said it was the unwanted child of a very poor woman. Supposedly, she'd cursed her thirteenth child, turning it into a monster.

Later, other people suggested it might be a still-living prehistoric animal. But no one has ever seen any other kind of animal—alive or dead—that looks anything like the Jersey Devil.

The creature is described as being about three and a half feet tall. They say it has a head like a horse, a long neck, and wings. Its back feet are hooves, and its front feet are paws. Some say it barks, but others have only heard it scream.

Among old records is a report made by Commodore Stephen Decatur, a naval hero. He was on a firing range when he saw a strange creature flying across the sky. He claims that he hit the creature with a cannon ball. *But it kept on flying.*

Napoleon Bonaparte's brother also

wrote about seeing the Jersey Devil while he was hunting in New Jersey.

During one week in January 1909, more than 1,000 people saw the creature! In fact, the Jersey Devil left tracks all over South Jersey and Philadelphia. In one town, strange hoof prints in the snow appeared. The prints went up trees and moved from roof to roof. And they disappeared in the middle of roads and fields—as if the creature had suddenly taken to the air. Trappers were called in to follow and capture the creature. None of them had seen tracks like those before.

All week long, the Jersey Devil killed chickens and dogs. It also terrorized people.

After 1909, the number of sightings reported to the authorities began to fall off. Had the creature gone away? Or died? Perhaps people *did* see it, but were worried that the authorities would think they were crazy.

Is the Jersey Devil a grotesque animal

of some kind? A hysterical burst of imagination? Or is it just a hoax? The great number of sightings and the tracks left in the snow are hard to deny.

On the other hand, nothing seems to be able to kill it. In 1909, the Jersey Devil flew into the power lines above the tracks of the electric railroad. After a witness reported a loud explosion, it was found that 20 feet of track had melted in both directions! No body was ever found, but the Jersey Devil appeared later . . . in very good health.

So is the Jersey Devil a natural or supernatural being? Whatever it is, given the large number of witnesses, the people of New Jersey have definitely seen *something*.

THE GHOST WHO
LOVED TO DANCE

"I must be the luckiest guy alive," Jerry Palus thought. He gazed at the beautiful girl in his arms as they whirled around the dance floor. She smiled and put her head on his shoulder.

The year was 1939—a long time ago. In those days public ballrooms were very popular places. Since Jerry loved to dance, he often went to the ballrooms. It was a great way to meet new girls.

Tonight he was dancing with the most fascinating girl he'd ever met. She said her first name was Mary, but she wouldn't tell him her last name. She was a gorgeous creature with blue eyes and curly blonde hair. Her pretty white ball gown made her look like a movie star. Just one thing seemed a little strange. Her hands were *very* cold. And once—

when Jerry kissed her—he couldn't help shivering. Even her *lips* were cold!

After the last dance, Mary told Jerry where she lived. "Could you give me a ride home?" she asked. "And would you mind driving down Archer Avenue before you take me home?"

Jerry was puzzled. Archer Avenue wasn't anywhere near Mary's house. But, hey—he really liked this girl. If that was what she wanted, why not?

As they drove down Archer Avenue, Jerry saw that they were approaching Resurrection Cemetery. Mary looked up when they neared the gates. "Stop here," she said. "I have to get out."

Jerry was confused, but he pulled over to the curb and parked. He started to open his door, but Mary stopped him. "No, Jerry, just drop me off here, okay? I have to say goodbye now," she said firmly. "Where I'm going, you can't follow."

Before Jerry could say another word, Mary leaped out of the car and ran toward the cemetery's tall, wrought iron gates. *Then she vanished!* Stunned, Jerry wondered if he'd been dancing with a ghost!

The next day Jerry drove to the address Mary had given him. A middle-aged woman answered his knock at the door. She invited him in and listened to his story. As Jerry talked, he glanced around the room. A photograph of Mary was on the table!

"There!" he said excitedly, pointing to the framed picture. "That's her. That's the girl I danced with last night."

The woman recoiled in shock. "What are you saying?" she cried out. "That's our daughter. You *couldn't* have danced with her last night, young man. She died five years ago."

* * * *

In later years Jerry Palus's pretty dance partner came to be known as "Resurrection Mary." She's one of Chicago's most famous ghosts. Some people call Mary's story an *urban myth—*

an often-repeated tale that grows and changes as it's passed along. Yet nobody has ever been able to trace the story back to its true source.

Most ghost stories are probably urban myths. What makes Mary's story different? Two things: The number of believable eyewitnesses, and the physical evidence some say she left behind.

The first story about Mary was told in 1934. Supposedly, she and her boyfriend were dancing at a ballroom on Archer Avenue. Sometime during the evening, Mary stormed out after an argument. As the story goes, she was hitchhiking down Archer Avenue when she was struck and killed by a hit-and-run driver. Her grieving family supposedly had her buried in Resurrection Cemetery.

Then, in 1939, she went dancing again—this time with Jerry Palus. He was the first person to get a close look at her ghost. But he wouldn't be the last.

Ralph, a cab driver, saw Mary's ghost

next. On a cold January night, Ralph had just dropped off a passenger. When he turned onto Archer Avenue, he spotted a young blonde woman wearing a frilly white dress. "She was standing there with no coat pointing up Archer Avenue," Ralph reported.

Thinking she might have had car trouble, he stopped and offered her a ride. She nodded her thanks and climbed in. As he pulled into traffic, Ralph asked why she was out alone on such a cold, dark night. But the pretty blonde just smiled in response. Then she pointed up Archer Avenue again.

She didn't say a word until the cab reached Resurrection Cemetery. Then she cried out, "Here! *Here!*"

Startled, Ralph hit the brakes. He looked all around for a house or an apartment building. But nothing was there except the cemetery.

When Ralph glanced back at his passenger, she'd disappeared!

Over the years, more people claimed to have seen Mary. Some said she dashed into the street in front of their cars. The drivers were certain they'd hit her. But when they got out of their cars, there was no body in the street.

Some people say they've seen Mary lying by the road, an apparent hit-and-run victim. But when the ambulance arrives, the injured girl has mysteriously disappeared. On some especially snowy nights, though, the imprint of a body can still be seen in the snow!

Other drivers on Archer Avenue say they've seen a girl dancing alone by the side of the road. Apparently, Mary's ghost still likes to dance.

As for physical evidence, even non-believers have trouble explaining this version of the story: In 1976, the police answered an emergency call. A young woman had accidentally been locked inside Resurrection Cemetery! But when the officer arrived, he couldn't find her.

What he did find, however, shook him badly. Two iron bars on one of the gates had been pried apart and badly burned. Stranger yet, a pair of human handprints were embedded in the metal! No one has ever been able to explain what had happened to the bars.

That spring, cemetery officials had the damaged bars blow-torched. The ugly burn marks were erased, but the handprints in the metal were still there. Eventually, the ruined bars were replaced with new ones.

So *be very careful* if you ever decide to check out Chicago's Archer Avenue and the Resurrection Cemetery. And *never* go there on a cold winter night. Who knows—you might find yourself dancing with a ghost!

STRANGE BUT TRUE STORIES

KILLER LAKES

Ephriam Che was feeling uneasy. "Something is wrong," he told himself as he headed downhill toward the village. "Something is very, very wrong."

Che lived in a mud-brick house on a cliff above Lake Nyos in Africa. The lake happens to be in a volcanic crater.

About 9 o'clock the night before, Che had been startled by a strange rumbling noise. It sounded like a rockslide. But when he stepped outside, it was too dark to see what was happening. All he could make out was a strange white mist rising from the lake. Later, when he went to bed, the healthy young man felt sick.

Che rushed to the village at first light, eager to check on his family. Normally, the air would have been filled with noise. Che should have heard the sounds of people laughing and talking, birds singing, and insects buzzing. But this morning there was only silence. That's when Che knew that his hunch had been right. Something terrible had happened.

The awful silence wasn't the only warning. The lake itself, usually sparkling blue, had turned a dull red color—and the waterfall was dry!

Che panicked. In the center of the village he made a ghastly discovery. Almost every villager was dead— including his parents, his brothers and sisters, and his aunts and uncles!

And people weren't the only victims. All the birds, insects, and wild animals in the area were dead, too. The death toll also included the villagers' farm animals and the plants around the lake. Dead fish floated on top of the water.

Che thought the end of the world had come. "All I remember is crying, crying, crying," he said later.

* * *

The date was August 21, 1986. That

day, more than 1,700 people seemed to have died instantly around Lake Nyos. But what had killed them? Was it the same thing that killed 17 people at another crater lake in Africa—Monoun—just two years before?

Scientists had found some important clues when they investigated the tragedy at Monoun. The water in the lake was loaded with carbon dioxide gas! Monoun had become a "killer lake."

Carbon dioxide gas—also called CO_2—is what makes your soda pop fizz. And this gas has other uses as well. For one thing, it's used in fire extinguishers. CO_2 puts out fires by smothering them.

In small amounts, CO_2 isn't harmful. But the huge amount of CO_2 that exploded out of Lake Nyos sucked the oxygen from the air. The people and animals couldn't breathe. Like a fire being squirted with a fire extinguisher, they were smothered.

In a killer lake, the gas comes from the

volcano underneath. Usually, the weight of the water traps the gas at the bottom of the lake. But that all changes when the pressure continues to build and build.

Think about it: If you shake a bottle of soda before you open it, the pressure builds. When you open the bottle, soda shoots out. In effect, that was what happened at the killer lakes.

What caused the release of so much CO_2 gas? Scientists thought it might have had something to do with a change in water temperature. So what could be done to keep it from happening again?

Engineers went to work on the problem. They finally figured out how to draw off the gas gradually. Pipes were installed in the lake. Now, small amounts of gas are rising through the pipes and being released in the air above.

But not *all* problems with the killer lakes have been solved. For one thing, the cost of drawing off the gas is very high. How can poor countries afford it?

And how many killer lakes might there be in the world? Scientists have already discovered another African lake similar to Monoun and Nyos. That's Lake Kivu in East Africa. No one knows how many more lakes might be killers. The number might be staggering.

HISTORIC VAMPIRES

WAS THERE A REAL DRACULA?

When we hear the word *vampire,* most of us think of Dracula. Most of us have seen the horror movies about this famous blood-sucker.

The fictional character called Dracula first appeared in a book by Bram Stoker. But where did Stoker get the idea?

Vampire stories have been around for hundreds of years. Most countries have their own myths and legends about vampires. But Bram Stoker based his story on a *real* person—Vlad Dracula, better known in history as Vlad the Impaler.

In 1431, Vlad Dracula was born in Sighisoara, a town in Transylvania. Today Transylvania is part of Romania. The name Dracula, by the way, comes from the Romanian word *drac* meaning "dragon." *Dracula* means "son of the dragon."

In 1451, Vlad's father was killed.

Determined to take revenge for his father's death, Vlad impaled his father's murderers on sharp stakes. This terrible act earned him the name of *Tepes*, which means "The Impaler."

In a lifetime of bloodshed and war, he continued to murder his enemies. Legend has it that he impaled 20,000 people in one day!

Vlad was assassinated in 1476.

Today, more than 500 years later, a Dracula theme park is being planned in Transylvania. When it is completed, the park is supposed to include amusement rides and a golf course. What do you suppose The Impaler would say if he knew he'd become a tourist attraction?

ELIZABETH BATHORY, THE QUEEN OF BLOOD

One of history's most scandalous criminals was Elizabeth Bathory, a vain and beautiful woman. Her ghastly deeds rival those of the worst serial killers ever known. She has been classified as a vampire because she was known to bite her victims and bathe in their blood.

Elizabeth was born into a rich and powerful family in 1560. At 15, she married Count Ferencz Nadasdy. Elizabeth had always been a cruel and sadistic person. While the Count was away at war, she discovered that she particularly enjoyed torturing her servants.

After her husband died, she worried about looking old. Somehow she became convinced that fresh blood would keep her looking young and beautiful. To provide for her daily blood bath, more than 600 women were murdered.

In 1610, the authorities investigated the count's widow. What they learned about her horrified them.

Yet because of her royal standing, Elizabeth could not be brought to trial. Instead, she was isolated in a small room in her castle. Only a tiny opening was provided so that food could be passed to her. After four years in that room, she died in 1614.

STRANGE BUT TRUE STORIES

ROCKS ON THE RUN?

Can a 700-pound boulder move along a flat surface on its own?

That's the mystery of a place called Racetrack Playa, a flat, old lakebed in Death Valley National Park. There, rocks of all shapes and sizes seem to be sliding across the dried lakebed by themselves. No one denies that they *do* move, but none of the investigators can agree on what *makes* them move.

Some scientists think the rocks are propelled by the wind. It's true that very fierce winds blow across Racetrack Playa. But other scientists don't buy that explanation. One study showed that it would take winds blowing at 500 miles per hour to move the rocks. *And winds that strong have never been recorded anywhere on earth.*

Another theory is that after it rains or

snows, the rocks move because the ground becomes very slippery. *But the rocks move no matter what the weather is like.*

Adding to the mystery, the rocks don't always move in a straight line. Sometimes they zigzag, and at other times they actually turn and change directions! Furthermore, all the rocks in the same location don't always move in the same direction at the same time.

Strangest of all: In the 90 years since the moving rocks were first discovered, no one has ever *seen* them move! Observers know the rocks *do* move because they leave a trail in the dirt behind them. Larger boulders can form trails up to 200 feet long. Smaller, lighter rocks sometimes move more than 600 feet!

Who knows? Maybe if *you* visit Death Valley's Racetrack Playa, you'll be the first person to see the rocks move!

STRANGE
BUT TRUE STORIES

TYPHOID MARY

Imagine you have a new job. You work hard, hoping to get ahead. One day a stranger comes to your workplace and accuses you of being a cold-blooded killer. He says your weapon is the horrible disease you're carrying!

If this sounds crazy, that's just what Mary Mallon thought when she was accused of being a killer.

In 1869, Mary was born in Ireland. She came to this country when she was 15. She was not educated, but she worked hard. Mary was such a good cook that she was soon in great demand.

One day a stranger showed up at the home where Mary was working. Barging into the kitchen, he accused her of spreading disease and killing people. He demanded that she give him samples of her blood, her urine, and her feces.

Mary was shocked. She'd never harmed anyone in her life. And besides, she felt perfectly healthy. Was this man crazy? Grabbing a carving fork, she threatened him with it if he didn't leave at once. The stranger hurriedly ran out of the house.

In fact, the stranger was a man named George Soper. He was investigating an outbreak of typhoid fever in another family—the Warrens. This deadly disease is spread through water or food sources. For example, if a sick person doesn't wash his hands before handling food, his germs can be spread to other people.

Soper knew that Mary had worked as a cook for the Warrens. He'd also learned that typhoid fever had broken out everywhere else she'd worked. Soper was sure that Mary was a typhoid carrier. Carriers are people who carry a disease in their bodies and pass it on to others.

From 1900 to 1907, Mary had worked as a cook for seven families. Twenty-two people in those families had become sick. And one young girl had died.

Even though Mary scared Soper off the first time, he didn't give up. Instead, he turned to the New York City Health Department for help. It took a visit from the police to finally capture Mary. They took her—kicking and screaming—to a hospital.

Typhoid germs were found in Mary's bodily fluids. She was sent to live in a cottage on the grounds of Riverside Hospital. Even though she hadn't broken any laws, she was held there without a trial.

Mary didn't understand. Since she felt fine, she believed the health department was being unfair.

For two years, health officials kept testing more samples. Most were positive. They showed that she was still a carrier. But when Mary sent samples to a private lab, they all came back negative.

In 1909, Mary Mallon sued the health

department. At the trial, the judge ruled against her. But in 1910, a new health commissioner decided she could go free. She was, however, forbidden to work as a cook again. Mary agreed.

Unfortunately, she still didn't believe that she was a carrier. She felt healthy, so how could she be carrying a deadly disease?

In 1915, typhoid fever broke out at Sloane Maternity Hospital in Manhattan. Twenty-five people became ill. Two died! The evidence pointed to a new cook named Mrs. Brown. This was a false name being used by Mary Mallon.

This time no one felt sorry for her. She'd deliberately put others at risk by going back to work as a cook. Mary was sent to her little cottage for the rest of her life. She died there in 1938.

But why was Mary the only carrier isolated for life? Other carriers had caused more illnesses and deaths than Mary. At least one of them had broken the law just as Mary had. So why was she punished so harshly?

Some people believe that it had to do with Mary herself. She was Irish. Many people were prejudiced against the Irish 100 years ago. Was it because she was a poor woman who was only a servant? Was it because of her bad temper?

Whatever the reasons, Mary Mallon has earned a place in history as the infamous "Typhoid Mary."

STRANGE BUT TRUE STORIES

SUNKEN CITIES

You may have heard stories about the fabled island of Atlantis. According to Plato, a great empire once existed there. He wrote that a single day and night of earthquakes and floods caused Atlantis to disappear below the waves.

Are stories of submerged cities only fairytales? Or could there be some truth to them?

STRUCTURES NEAR CUBA

In the year 2000, Canadian and Cuban explorers found the remains of a sunken city off the coast of Cuba. The explorers were using sonar to look for lost treasure ships. Instead they discovered an ancient underwater city—complete with its roads, buildings, and pyramids.

The explorers showed scientists their videotapes of the structures. One expert said that the tape clearly shows symbols and writing carved into the stone. But as yet no one has been able to identify the language.

In 1966, scientists dug up a huge stone structure on Cuba's west coast. Found near the sunken city, the structure is estimated to be about 6,000 years old. Scientists agree that the underwater city is just about the same age.

AN ANCIENT EGYPTIAN PORT

Another underwater city has been found off the coast of Egypt. Scholars think it might once have been Egypt's main port city in the time of the pharaohs. Researchers suspect the city sank when an earthquake rocked the region about 1,000 years ago.

Even though the city is underwater, it is in very good condition. Huge statues, gold coins, and pieces of jewelry have been recovered there.

JAPAN'S SUBMERGED STRUCTURES

Japan has its own underwater cities stretching over 311 miles of ocean floor! Huge sunken pyramids were first discovered by divers near Okinawa. Initially, it was thought that the stone structures had been carved by nature. New evidence, however, suggests that people may have built them.

Researchers have identified stone terraces, walls, and stone columns. They also found roads, stone steps, and what looks like postholes that could have supported wooden structures. On nearby land, there are structures with the same kind of building design. These are the clues that have led some scientists to think the monuments were manmade.

No one is sure how to date these monuments. They may have been built 10,000 years ago.

INDIA'S OLDEST CIVILIZATION?

A huge underwater city found off

the western coast of India is surprising historians and scientists. Scholars had always thought that the 4,000-year-old Harappan civilization was the oldest one in India. But the underwater city in the Gulf of Cambay turned out to be more than 9,000 years old.

Scientists have had good evidence to study. They've found sections of walls, construction materials, pottery, beads, sculpture, and human bones and teeth. These materials have been found to be almost 9,500 years old.

India's sunken city is about five miles long and approximately two miles wide. It was discovered in 2002.

PERU'S UNDERWATER TEMPLE

In 2000, the ruins of an ancient temple were found in Peru. It is located at the bottom of Lake Titicaca, the world's highest lake. Divers there also found a terrace once used for farming, a long road, and a wall about 2,600 feet long.

Scientists believe the ruins are 1,000 to 1,500 years old.

For generations, local people have told fascinating stories about what might lay at the bottom of the lake. One legend tells of Inca gold lost by the Spanish. These tales of treasure brought the famous French oceanographer Jacques Cousteau to the lake. But the treasure he found was only ancient pottery. So perhaps the gold is still there, just waiting to be discovered.

* * *

All over the world explorers and scientists are finding sunken cities. Some are so old that books about our ancient history may have to be rewritten!

Who knows? Perhaps today's expert explorers will even find Atlantis!

STRANGE BUT TRUE STORIES

COLMA—CITY OF THE DEAD

Colma, California—just south of San Francisco—is the only city in the world where the dead outnumber the living. In the year 2000, there were 1,191 people living in Colma. But more than a million people are buried there.

Colma is tiny. It covers only 2.25 square miles in size. Yet there are 14 cemeteries within the city limits! People are buried in all the graveyards—except Pet's Rest, which is a cemetery for animals. Pet's Rest gets more donations of flowers every day than any other cemetery in Colma.

The strangest thing buried in Pet's Rest is not a pet. It's a cake! Its owner kept the cake for several years. Finally the cake was pronounced dead. Then, for some unknown reason, its owner had it buried in an unmarked grave.

How did Colma become a city of the dead? In the mid-1800s, Colma was just a small settlement. Then, seven years later, Holy Cross Cemetery was established in the area. Ten years after that, the people of San Francisco realized that graveyards were using up too much costly real estate. So they passed a law forbidding anyone else from being buried inside the San Francisco city limits. From then on, the dead were moved south—to Colma.

But San Franciscans didn't stop there. In 1914, they decided that even people who were already buried would have to be moved elsewhere.

Most were against digging up the dead. They fought the idea until 1940. Then people got greedy. They agreed that most of the cemeteries in San Francisco occupied valuable land. So there was a mass departure of the dead from San Francisco. From one cemetery alone, the remains of 35,000 pioneers were trucked to Colma.

Usually, there isn't much excitement in Colma. But in 1971, the gravediggers, gardeners, and other workers there went out on strike. The strike lasted four months. During that time, more than 1,800 bodies had to be stored in funeral homes all over the Bay Area. After the strike ended, it took nearly two months to bury all the bodies.

Colma's economy depends mainly on cemetery workers. But Colma has other businesses as well—such as restaurants, car dealerships, clothing stores, and real estate offices. There's even a golf course—sandwiched in between two cemeteries.

Colma offers visitors interesting things to do. Cypress Lawn—one of the oldest and best-known cemeteries—offers both bus and walking tours. You can also picnic in some of the cemeteries—unless the thought of eating lunch in a graveyard bothers you. Perhaps you'd like to visit the rose garden in Woodlawn cemetery. But be warned! Some people like to sprinkle the ashes of their cremated family members in the garden. The roses are very healthy, but don't be surprised if you see bits of bone scattered across the ground.

One of the most popular pastimes in Colma is reading epitaphs on headstones. Many famous people are buried there: Wyatt Earp, the famous lawman who cleaned up Tombstone, Arizona. Famous newspaperman William Randolph Hearst. Even Tina Turner's dog is buried in Colma!

With all these wonderful things to do in the City of Cemeteries, it's easy to understand Colma's motto: "It's good to be alive in Colma. "

STRANGE BUT TRUE STORIES

KURU—THE GHOST DISEASE

Everyone knew the fate of the little girl shivering by the fire. Soon she wouldn't be able to eat, and then she'd be paralyzed. Finally she would die! She was suffering from a disease called *kuru*, which was becoming an epidemic. No one knew how to stop it.

It was 1955. The child was a member of a primitive tribe called the Fore who lived on a remote island. Papua New Guinea is about 100 miles north of Australia. The Fore lived high in the mountains there. The men hunted, while the women planted taro and sweet potatoes. They were a superstitious people who believed in sorcery and ghosts. *Kuru* was making many ghosts!

The Fore believed that *kuru* was the result of a curse. The local doctor didn't believe in sorcery. He thought *kuru* must be a rare disease. It might even be a new disease no one had seen before. But what caused it? A virus? Genetics? Or was it passed through infectious bacteria?

The doctor sent blood and tissue samples to a lab in Australia. They came back normal. His efforts to grow viruses in the lab failed. After two years of hard work, he still had no clue what *kuru* was. People continued to pour into the local hospital. Their families could only watch helplessly as their loved ones died.

Then, in 1957, a young American scientist arrived in Papua New Guinea. He had come to visit a friend but also to learn more about *kuru*. He'd read about the disease but didn't believe what he'd read. When he saw the victims, he was stunned. He immediately joined in the effort to help solve the mystery.

After months of studying the disease, the doctor and the scientist were still no closer to understanding its cause. The American felt there was something he'd overlooked. So he started over. He made careful lists of everything that might have something to do with the disease.

On one of his lists he wrote the word *cannibalism*. Knowing that at one time the Fore had practiced cannibalism, he'd been assured they no longer did. But was that true? And could it have anything to do with the disease?

In 1959, the doctor and the scientist read an article. It pointed out the similarities between *kuru* and a disease called "scrapie." Scrapie occurred in sheep. If brain tissue from a sick sheep was injected into a healthy animal, the healthy sheep got scrapie, too.

The doctors in Papua New Guinea decided to try an experiment. They injected brain tissue from people who had died of *kuru* into chimpanzees. It took several years, but eventually the chimps all came down with *kuru*.

The doctors were stunned. *Kuru* was indeed a virus, a very slow-moving virus.

Now they realized that the first Fore victims had been infected many years before. But how had they caught it in the first place?

Two anthropologists came up with the answer. In 1915, the Fore had visited another tribe—the Kamano—in the north. That was when the Kamano people introduced the Fore to cannibalism.

Since then, the Fore had made cannibalism a funeral ritual. When one of them died, the rest of the tribe cooked and ate his flesh. If he had *kuru*, they consumed it.

Today, the Fore no longer practice cannibalism—and *kuru* is no longer making ghosts.

PHANTOM SHIPS

NOVA SCOTIA'S BURNING GHOST SHIP

One evening a handful of men stood talking near the harbor in Cape John, Nova Scotia. Suddenly, one of them pointed toward the channel. Glancing up, the others, too, saw an old-fashioned sailing ship. It was ablaze from one end to the other!

The men knew there was no hope for the ship. But maybe they could rescue some of the crew. Quickly boarding a small boat, they rowed as fast as they could toward the burning ship. But a mist was rising, and soon it would be dark. Could they reach the survivors in time?

They didn't have to worry. The burning ship vanished right before their eyes! The sailing vessel they had seen was a *ghost ship*.

The burning ghost ship has been

spotted many times by dozens of people. No one knows what causes it to appear. Is it really a phantom ship? Or is it only an optical illusion?

A BAD OMEN: *THE FLYING DUTCHMAN*

The most famous phantom ship is *The Flying Dutchman*. (That name, by the way, refers to the captain, not the ship.)

One stormy night in 1680, a Dutch ship was in trouble. It was trying to sail around the Cape of Good Hope at the tip of Africa during a fierce storm. The stubborn captain was determined to fight the storm and sail on. Although the crew begged him to turn back, he refused. Instead, to their horror, he shook his fist at the heavens. He shouted that he would sail around the Cape even if it took until the end of time.

In minutes the ship sank, drowning all hands onboard. But the captain's punishment for being so stubborn was to sail the seas forever!

You might think that this is only a legend—except for one thing. Many reliable witnesses claim to have actually seen *The Flying Dutchman!*

One of the first recorded sightings was in 1835. The captain of a British ship wrote about it. He said that *The Flying Dutchman* sailed so close the crew was afraid the two ships would collide.

In 1881, a young midshipman wrote in the ship's log about seeing *The Flying Dutchman*. That young man was a prince who later became King George V of England.

In 1939, there was another sighting. Dozens of people enjoying the beach on the coast of South Africa said they saw the ghost ship. Their vividly detailed descriptions of the ghostly ship were reported in local newspapers.

During World War II, sailors on a German submarine also claimed to have seen *The Flying Dutchman*. And in 1959, the crew of a freighter reported a near collision with the ghost ship.

Many sailors believe that it's a bad omen to see *The Flying Dutchman*. In some cases, sailors who spot the phantom die suddenly and mysteriously. In 1881, for example, seeing *The Flying Dutchman*, a sailor fell from the rigging to his death. So beware!

THE *BAYCHINCO*

In 1931, a freighter named the *Baychinco* got stuck in the thick Alaskan ice. The crew stayed aboard, waiting for the ice to break up. But then a severe storm hit the area. Winds howled and blinding snow fell. Waves rocked the ship so violently the crew was afraid the ship might break up.

The captain ordered everyone to abandon ship. The crew climbed off the ship and lay flat on the solid sheet of ice. There they waited for the storm to end.

When the storm was finally over, the sailors were shocked by what they saw.

The *Baychinco* had vanished! Had the ship broken up and sunk? Not a trace of wreckage could be seen. Finally, the crew decided only one thing could have happened. The winds had broken the ship loose from the ice, and it had drifted free.

But the story doesn't end there. From that day on the *Baychinco* has been a "ghost ship," drifting aimlessly among the packs of Arctic ice. For many years, people have tried to find the *Baychinco*. Why? Because it carried a valuable cargo of furs. But no one has had any luck.

To be sure, the ship has been seen— but always at a distance. Often it is shrouded in fog or rain or snow. And worse yet, the ice packs prevent any other ship from getting close to it.

Perhaps the *Baychinco* is indeed a ghost ship.

HORRORS IN THE WAX MUSEUM

LITTLE MARIE AND THE DEATH MASKS

Marie Gosholtz peered into the growing darkness and shuddered. The sights and smells of death were all around her. No matter how often she visited, she never got over the horror.

"Don't think about it," she scolded herself. "Just find the head!"

She raised her lantern higher. A pile of bodies without heads and heads without bodies covered the floor. Marie knew that the head of France's queen must lay somewhere in that tangle of broken corpses. Marie Antoinette had just been executed.

* * *

The year was 1793 and the place was France. The event in progress was the French Revolution—better known by its thousands of victims as *The Terror*.

Marie herself had nearly become one of those victims. She and her mother had been arrested and imprisoned. For many months she had been terrified that they would die on the guillotine. This terrible "murdering machine" was the official instrument of execution during the revolution. It killed its victims by quickly and efficiently chopping off their heads.

But at the last minute, Marie was freed from prison. Why? Because she had a very special talent. She knew how to make death masks!

Before cameras were invented, a death mask was the best way to portray a person's true features. This was a plaster of Paris mold of the deceased person's face. When the mold was dried it was filled with wax to make a likeness of the face.

Marie made the death masks of many well-known people who were executed during the French Revolution. In time, she also learned to make entire wax figures. Her teacher, Dr. Curtius, left his collection of life-size wax figures to Marie when he died.

Later, Marie married. Now Madame Tussaud, she took her collection of wax figures to London. There she started a business that would become famous—Madame Tussaud's Wax Museum.

Today there are Madame Tussaud's Wax Museums all over the world. Many celebrities—from movie stars to politicians—pose for the artists and have *life* masks made. It's considered an honor to be a wax figure in Madame Tussaud's.

In London, one display in the Chamber of Horrors portrays little Marie Gosholtz. She's shown searching for the head of Marie Antoinette.

THE RESENTFUL TAX COLLECTOR

In 1857, Richard Turner, an American businessman, visited Madame Tussaud's Wax Museum in London. He was very impressed. "I've got a great idea," he thought. "Why don't I build a wax museum in Sacramento, California?" Because of the gold rush, hundreds of newcomers were pouring into town every day. A wax museum would surely be very popular.

The centerpiece of his new show was a scene from the French Revolution. Posed near the infamous guillotine were several wax figures. They represented actual people who'd been beheaded during the Revolution. The scene included one pale-faced man in a black suit. In life, he'd been a ruthless tax collector who made himself rich by cheating poor people out of their money.

The Sacramento museum was an instant success. But shortly after it opened, the janitor told Turner an unsettling story. "Somehow," he said, "the figure of the tax collector is—uh, moving around at night. And worse yet, its head keeps falling off!"

When the museum closed for the night, Turner made sure the door to the display was locked. And he hired an extra guard to patrol the building. But his efforts did no good. At some time during the night, someone—or some thing—had moved the wax figure.

Turner and the janitor were stumped. They decided to spend the night in the room to keep watch over the guillotined figures. A little before 2:30 A.M. they were startled to see the figure of the tax collector move. They stared in horror as first the arms, then the legs, and then the wax face slowly seemed to come alive. Then, as its eyebrows came together in a frown, the figure spoke. "Is it not possible to get some peace at night? More than 50 years ago, people came to watch us die. Now more people are coming to see our spirits encased in wax. We've had enough! Come here no more during the hours of darkness, or you will regret it."

When the story leaked out, a Sacramento newspaper reporter visited the museum. He asked if he could spend a night in the horror chamber, and Turner agreed.

The young man was locked into the room the next night. Outside the door, the janitor stood guard—just in case. But after a few hours he dozed off!

It was 2:31 A.M. when a series of horrible screams and a frantic pounding on the door awakened the janitor. He stumbled to the door and unlocked it as quickly as he could. The terrified reporter fell into his arms in a dead faint.

Later, the reporter wrote an account of what had happened. He said that, in the dim light, the wax figures looked very lifelike. The scene was eerie, but not truly frightening—until he noticed something that made his skin crawl. Every time he looked away from the tax collector and back again, the figure seemed to have moved. So he gazed steadily at the wax figure for a couple of minutes. To his horror, he saw one arm begin to move—slowly at first, then faster. Suddenly the tax collector pulled off its own head and dropped it on the floor! Then the headless body began to stagger toward the reporter, with its arms outstretched.

The wax figure continued to lurch forward as the reporter backed up. When the reporter reached the door, he screamed and began pounding on the door. Just as the reporter heard the key turning in the lock, the cold wax fingers were closing around his throat.

The next morning the tax collector's head was found on the floor near the other figures. But the body lay near the door. And its wax fingers were strangely flat and bent out of shape.

A few days later, the figure of the tax collector was melted down and replaced with a new figure. That put an end to the ghostly disturbances. The museum continued to be successful until 1885.

Do you think the reporter made up his story—perhaps to attract more visitors to the museum? If so, think again. His story wasn't published until long after his death in the 1930s.

MYSTERIOUS DISAPPEARANCES

GONE IN THE BLINK OF AN EYE

Let's face it—people disappear. It happens all the time. But sooner or later there's usually a good explanation.

But can you imagine someone disappearing before your very eyes? How would you explain *that*?

In 1854, a farmer in Selma, Alabama, disappeared as four witnesses watched. Orion Williamson got up from his chair on the porch of his farmhouse. He set off across the field to bring his horses in from the pasture. His wife and child were watching him from the porch. On the other side of the field, two of his neighbors were riding by. They waved at Orion.

Then, suddenly, before their very eyes, Orion vanished.

The witnesses searched the field for hours, but *there was no trace of him.*

People from town came to help out. They brought bloodhounds, but the searchers and the dogs couldn't find Orion either. He was never found! To this day, no one knows what happened to Orion Williamson.

VANISHED INTO THIN AIR

Another strange disappearance took place in 1937. The victims were Amelia Earhart—a famous woman pilot—and her co-pilot, Fred Noonan.

In 1928, Amelia Earhart became the first woman pilot to fly across the Atlantic Ocean.

On May 20, 1937, she and Noonan took off from California to fly around the world. Everything went well until July 2. That morning Earhart and Noonan left New Guinea. Their destination was tiny Howland Island in the middle of the Pacific. Near Howland Island, a Coast

Guard cutter was waiting to send homing signals to the small plane.

But Amelia's plane never made it!

Some people were sure she'd crashed at sea. Others were certain she'd been forced down on a small coral island. But a massive search didn't turn up a single clue. There was no trace of the famous woman pilot.

To this day, the fate of the daring aviator remains a mystery.

PORTLAND'S TERRIBLE SHANGHAI TUNNELS

Portland, Oregon, is a busy modern city. It's famous for the beautiful gardens that helped earn it the nickname "City of Roses."

But there's a darker side to Portland's history. Years ago that "other Portland" earned the city a very different nickname. Sailors from near and far called it "The Worst Port in the World." Why? Because of what lay underground.

In the 1800s, Portland was a busy waterfront town. Ships arrived every day, bringing in goods. Others departed with cargoes of lumber and grains. To keep up the heavy flow of traffic, the sea captains needed cheap labor. For that they relied on men known as "crimps."

Crimps hung around boarding houses along the waterfront. When a man stopped for a meal or to find a place to stay, the crimp would be very friendly. He might buy the man a hot meal or a drink. Little did the newcomer know that his food or drink had been drugged. The moment he passed out, he was dropped through a trap door into a tunnel.

These were called "shanghai" tunnels because most of the ships sailed from Portland to Shanghai, China. The kidnapped victims who were sold to the sea captains were said to have been "shanghaied."

Small musty cells opened off the tunnels. The victims were held in these cells until they could be sold. Once the drugged man was dumped in a cell, the crimp took away his shoes or boots. Then the crimp scattered broken glass on the floor. A man with bare feet was less likely to walk around on broken glass. And if he did try to escape, his bloody footprints would make it easier for a crimp to track him down.

The sea captains paid about $50 for each victim. Before the victims were taken to the ship, they were drugged again. These "knock-out drops" didn't wear off until the ship was far out at sea. Now the kidnapped man had no way to escape. It took him six years—two full voyages—to get back to Portland.

Some say that about 1,500 men—and even some women—were kidnapped each year. Other people claim it was twice that number.

One of the worst crimps was a man named Joseph Kelly. He became famous for the way he cheated one sea captain. Kelly wrapped a 7-foot wooden statue in blankets. Then he sold it, along with a group of real victims, to a sea captain looking for sailors. Kelly warned the captain not to wake the drugged "man" until the ship was well out to sea.

When the captain tried to rouse the man, he discovered the statue! Furious at being cheated, he threw the statue overboard. And strangely enough, the wooden statue washed ashore in Oregon. It's now on display in Portland.

"Shanghaiing" was finally stopped in 1915.

For many years, Portland had turned its back on this ugly, dark page of its history. But Portland wasn't the only city to practice "shanghaiing." So did many other west coast cities, including San Francisco and Los Angeles. Still, by all accounts, Portland was the worst.

Today, the tunnels have been opened for tours. An underground museum is planned. But some things never change: Once again the tunnels are making money for the local economy.

STRANGE BUT TRUE STORIES

DINOSAURS LIVING IN AFRICA TODAY?

Did you see the movie *Jurassic Park*? The special effects made audiences feel like they were walking with real dinosaurs! But, of course, that's impossible. Everyone knows that dinosaurs were wiped out millions of years ago.

Or were they?

For some 200 years, strange reports have come out of Africa. They tell about huge creatures that resemble dinosaurs. They're said to live in a remote area of the Congo called the Likouala Swamp. This swamp covers about 55,000 square miles— and 80% of it has never been explored.

Different African tribes give different names to these animals. One is *mok`ele mbembe,* which means "river stopper." This animal is described as being about 30 feet long. It has smooth, brownish gray skin, and a long thin neck. The animal lives on a diet of plants.

What did scientists think when they first heard this description? Some thought it sounded very much like a *sauropod* dinosaur.

In 1932, a British scientist came across some huge footprints. That same year another scientist and an animal trader were paddling up a river in western Africa. Suddenly, they heard a terrifying sound—unlike anything they'd ever heard before. Then a lizard-like creature rose out of the water in front of their canoe. Later, the scientist wrote: *It looked like something that ought to have died out millions of years ago.*

In 1980, two scientists showed pictures of local animals to the natives. The natives correctly named each animal. But the last picture was that of a large dinosaur called an *apatosaurus*. Without hesitating, the natives identified it as *mok`ele mbembe,* an animal they knew.

So far no Westerners have personally seen the animals. They've only heard the stories told by the natives. In 1959, several people told western explorers they'd seen one of the creatures killed by natives at Lake Tele.

In 1988, a Congolese wildlife official traveled to Lake Tele with a Japanese expedition. The official reported that everyone saw the huge, humped back of an animal moving slowly in the shallow lake.

In 1992, another Japanese team supposedly filmed one of the animals from an airplane. The film—only 15 seconds long—shows a large but unidentifiable shape moving in the water.

In 2000, another expedition returned empty-handed. But believers point out that it's hard to get into the remote regions of the Congo.

Until the mystery is solved, however, more people will surely join the search for *mok`ele mbembe.*

STRANGE BUT TRUE STORIES

THE MYSTERIOUS BAGHDAD BATTERIES

Perhaps you've been taught that Count Alessandro Volta invented the electric battery in 1800. Right? Maybe not!

In 1936, a number of strange little clay jars were found near Baghdad, Iraq. They were discovered in the ruins of a 2,000-year-old village.

Inside each six-inch jar was a cylinder of sheet-copper containing an iron rod. Scientists determined that the iron rod had been partly eaten away by acid. They believed the acid had come from either wine or vinegar. Both the tops and bottoms of the jars were sealed with asphalt.

The archaeologist who examined the jars was amazed. They could be only one thing: batteries! But that couldn't be! How could ancient people have made batteries? And for what use?

In 1970, a German scientist built an exact replica of the Baghdad battery. He guessed that the ancient people would have used freshly squeezed grape juice for the acid.

Sure enough, the replica he built *did* produce electricity. It was less than a volt, but he used that energy to electroplate a silver statuette with gold. (To "electroplate" something is to transfer a thin layer of metal to its surface.)

Not everyone agrees that the ancient batteries were used for electroplating. Some think they might have been used to help stop pain. The Chinese had already developed acupuncture. They still use acupuncture with an electric current. This could explain the needle-like objects found in the same location as the batteries.

Whatever their use, the "Baghdad batteries" continue to mystify and amaze us. Perhaps we don't give ancient people enough credit for their discoveries!

STRANGE BUT TRUE STORIES

THE LIONS OF TSAVO— SAVAGE KILLERS OR ?

In 1898 the British decided to build a railroad in East Africa. Soon laborers started work on a railway bridge across the Tsavo River. But soon they ran into an unexpected problem: lions! And these weren't just any lions. These two burly cats were vicious man-eaters!

Night after night the huge beasts stalked their prey—the railroad workers. After silently creeping down from the hills, they would attack with savage fury.

Thorn fences were built around the camp, but the fences couldn't keep the lions out. Then huge fires were built to keep the lions away—but not even fire could turn away the killers.

Rumors ran like wildfire through the camp. The lions could not be stopped. They could not be killed. Surely they were evil spirits! The workers named the dreaded lions the *Ghost* and the *Darkness*.

As hundreds of workers fled Tsavo, work on the bridge came to a halt. John Patterson, the chief engineer, was worried. He knew that once the animals had tasted human flesh, they'd be likely to kill even more people. He'd have to figure out a way to destroy them.

Patterson erected a hunting platform outside the camp. At night he'd take his rifle, climb onto the platform, and wait for the lions to appear. One night, just as he was aiming at one of the lions, a passing owl hit him on the head! Luckily, he was able to regain his balance—but of course he missed the shot.

Another time his gun misfired. Once again he'd missed his chance to kill one of the rogue lions.

Finally, Patterson decided to build a huge, wooden trap. It was shaped like a large rectangular box. At one end, Patterson planned to place some workers as "bait." To protect them, he put bars in the middle of the trap. And he armed the men with rifles.

The trap worked! One of the lions sprang the trip wire and was trapped inside. The terrified workers fired wildly through the bars, but not a single shot hit the lion! In fact, one of the bullets actually broke a slat in the trap door. The enraged beast quickly made its escape.

Next, Patterson decided to track the lions to their den. The night before, the man-eaters had dragged away a bloody corpse. It wasn't hard for Patterson to follow the trail of bloody paw prints.

Eventually, he found a cave where he figured the lions might be hiding. Inside, he made a gruesome discovery. The floor of the cave was littered with human skulls and bones! Now Patterson was certain that this was the lions' den. Unfortunately, the lions were nowhere in the area that night.

A few days later, he finally shot and

killed one of the lions. The beast was nearly 10 feet long from its nose to the tip of its tail. It took eight men to carry the dead lion back to camp.

Three weeks later, Patterson managed to shoot and kill the other one. At last, the slaughter was over.

Once the lions were dead, the workers returned. Their reign of terror had lasted nine months. By some accounts, the lions had killed and devoured more than 130 men! The bridge was soon finished.

As for the lions, Patterson saved their skins and skulls. Later, he sold these grim souvenirs to Chicago's Field Museum of Natural History. A taxidermist stuffed the lions, and they're still on display there today.

Why were the *Ghost* and the *Darkness* such savage killers? Some say it's harder for animals to hunt when humans begin to move into their territory.

The scientists also made a very interesting discovery when they examined the Tsavo lions' skulls. One of the rogue lions had an injured jaw. That certainly made it difficult to hunt. Humans were easier than other animals to kill. Was that the answer? Maybe, maybe not. The scientists also pointed out that other lions with similar injuries did not become man-eaters.

A third theory is that once the lions had tasted human flesh, they simply preferred it. Perhaps they didn't *want* to eat anything else.

One thing is certain: The lions of Tsavo were not the first man-eaters, nor will they be the last. In the 1930s, a Bengal tiger in Nepal killed more than 400 people. And in 1991, another man-eating lion in Mfuwe, Zambia, was shot and killed. It measured ten-and-a-half feet from nose to tail. To this day, it is considered to be the largest man-eating lion ever recorded.

TULPAS—MIND CREATURES OF TIBET

Did you ever wish you could create a "perfect person"? A girlfriend, say, or a bodyguard?

In Tibet, creatures created in a person's mind are called *tulpas*. It isn't easy to create a *tulpa*. In most cases, those who produce these mind creatures are highly skilled magicians.

Creating a *tulpa* can also be dangerous. Consider, for example, the tulpa created by Alexandra David-Neel.

Alexandra was born in France in 1868. Even as a very young child, she loved adventure. When she grew up, she traveled through Asia. For a while she lived in Tibet. It was there she learned that Tibetans believe the natural and supernatural worlds exist together.

When Alexandra heard about *tulpas*,

she was both puzzled and fascinated. How could someone create a creature from his or her thoughts? And just how "real" would this creature be?

Alexandra decided she wanted to create a *tulpa* of her own. So she shut herself away where no one could interrupt her thoughts.

She decided to create a monk—one who was short, fat, and had a cheerful smile. For many months she meditated. Finally, she began to see a ghostly monk. In time, he became much like a guest in her apartment.

Some time later, Alexandra left on a trip. Along the way she was surprised to see that her *tulpa* had joined her party.

Soon something strange happened. She actually felt his hand touch her shoulder. And she noticed that he was undergoing a physical change. His round face was growing lean. His cheerful smile was turning into a crafty sneer.

One day a Tibetan herdsman brought

her a gift of butter. When he saw the monk in her tent, he thought he was looking at a living person.

Alexandra realized that she was no longer in control of her mind creature. He was beginning to have a life of his own!

This *tulpa* was now making her very nervous. He'd become her "day-nightmare," as she later put it.

Alexandra was planning a trip to Lhasa, the capital of Tibet. She didn't want her *tulpa* to come with her. So she decided to "dissolve" him. But that was easier said than done.

Alexandra had to go into seclusion— just as she'd done when she first created the creature. By using meditation and performing other rituals, she was finally able to dissolve the *tulpa*. But it took six months of hard work. Her mind-creature had a stubborn hold on life!